How to do Zen Meditat[ion]

By Kuriakos

© 2008 Kuriakos

All Rights Reserved

This book may not be reproduced in whole or part by electronic or other means without permission.

Printed in the USA

ISBN: 978-1-4357-3554-5

Table of Contents

Introduction:

I. What is Meditation?.......7

II. Where to do Meditation.......9

III. When to do Meditation.......11

IV. Why do Meditation?......13

V. How to do Meditation.......18

VI. Types of Meditation.......24

VII. The Zen Buddhist Meditation.......31

The Zen Buddhist Meditation Journal

Caveat

This text deals with astral and physical forces that can be dangerous if misused or used carelessly. It is important that the reader know his or her own physical, emotional, and psychological limits before undertaking the studies within this book. The exercises herein and techniques discussed are not to be used in lieu of the services of trained and qualified professionals such as physicians or psychologists. The reader is responsible, in every way, for his or her actions involved in using the rituals in this book and the author, publisher and the distributor of this text are not responsible for any undesirable outcomes from the use of this book.

List of Books by the Author

To buy more of the Author's books please go to www.**Kuriakos.biz**
Available in print and download versions.

How to Communicate with Spirits
The Enochian Angel's Ritual Book
How to Summons the 22 Letters of Hebrew
The Necronomicon Ritual Book
The Goetia Ritual Book
Astrology Magick
How to do Telekinesis and Energy Work
Tarot Magick
How to do Transcendental Meditation
How to do Past Life Regression
How to do Automatic Writing
The Fast Road to Enlightenment WorkBook
The Kabbalah Tree of Life Ritual Book
How to Summons the 72 Names of God
How to do Self-Hypnosis

Egyptian Magick
Greek and Roman Magick
The Modern Magick Ritual Book
Celtic Magick

And many more at www.**Kuriakos.biz**

Introduction

This book, How to do Zen Buddhist Meditation, is a very short to the point book on how to quickly and easily do Zen Buddhist Meditation anytime and anywhere. Zen Buddhist Meditation allows you to quiet the loud thinking conscious mind and access the subconscious mind to bring amazing peace into your life, to solve your life's problems and to get answers about ways to improve your life from the spiritual world and to greatly improve your health! Anyone from beginner to advance can easily do Zen Buddhist Meditation by following these very simple and effective meditations in this book. This book makes it so easy to do and requires no experience of any kind and will show you step by step how to quickly go into a Zen Buddhist Meditation. You will be able to get answers about your past, present or future situation in your life concerning money, relationships, health, spirituality and many more things as well. Over 20 years of experience has been accessed in this book to give you the most quick and effective method to Zen Buddhist Meditation and to see immediate results in your life.

I. What is Meditation?

Dhyana is the Sanskrit word meaning meditation and is about the process of quieting the mind to free it from any attachments, illusions or preconceptions. During meditation one will quiet the senses and go inward with a focus which is known in Sanskrit as Pratyahara. So meditation is simply quieting all your normal everyday senses you use to go inward and focus to allow the Universal energy, knowledge and spiritual insight to come through to you. Anyone can do meditation from young to old or beginner to advanced. Meditation is **not a religion** and is not based on a belief like a religion but instead is Universal in its concepts of energy and connectedness with all of us on the planet.

II. Where to do Meditation

The best place to do meditation is a place that you can call your temple. This place is where you won't be disturbed with the phone, computer or any electronic devices. A place where there is no talking or few noises to disturb you. This is your temple and place of ritual where do your meditations to find peace in your life and to listen to the answers that come through from The Universe or Source. Buy, make or use a small tiny end table as your altar. Put a nice silk or cloth you like on the altar and candles and sandalwood incense. Sandalwood incense calms the mind, body and spirit and is like a trigger for your mind. Every time you smell the sandalwood incense your mind will immediately know after a while that this is when its time to relax and do the meditation. This is like a trigger for your mind to put it immediately into the Alpha state brain wave which is what is needed to do effective meditation.

III. When to do Meditation

When to do meditation is entirely up to you. Are you a structured kind of person that always does things like clockwork? If this is you, then set a time to meditation preferably after work in the evening when you are winding down to help you be able to easily access this Alpha state needed for meditation. Are you a free-wheelin kind of person? If this you, then do meditation whenever you feel motivated to do it so your energy will be more focused and you will get the best benefits out of your meditations. Every person is unique in their daily rhythms and cycles of their body and energy so it's best in life to follow what works and feels best for you. You are the creator of your life so create an amazingly happy life for yourself by always doing things that make you feel better and happier.

IV. Why do Meditation?

Mediation has been proven over and over by science to drop the body into the alpha brain wave state. When you are awake and thinking your brain is in the beta brain wave state. Then when you go into a meditation your brain will 'drop' or slow down the cycles per second and drop to this alpha brain wave state. You can actually feel this drop in your brain. To test this out right now, close your eyes and visualize going down and elevator and count down 1 to 15. Below alpha brain wave state is theta and delta and this is where you are sleeping or in a coma. The alpha state not only relieves internal stress in the brain but also is the connection to the subconscious which is linked to the astral plane where spirits reside so we can communicate with the spiritual world in this way for answers. The alpha brain wave state also connects us to Source energy which is the God/all knowing energy and will manifest through our daily lives as instant thoughts that appear in our mind without even thinking about that subject at all. These thoughts from Source can be small like to move an appointment to another time or big as to a great insight for your life. Albert Einstein came up with most of his inventions from this alpha state. He would take a 15 minute nap and then after he woke up this insight from Source would come to him. When you sleep at night you are only accessing this alpha brain wave state for a few minutes as it's between when you lay down and get drowsy. So meditation is a far more effective way to access the alpha brain wave state as this allows you to be conscious and awake yet have the chatter mind go quiet to have a clear channel of insight and peacefulness for you life. You will know that you are in the alpha brain wave state or meditative state because your chatter mind which is thinking non stop will go silent and you will still be awake but yet not be actively thinking so much.

Here is a list of the many physical and mental benefits from meditation:

* Lowers stress in the body

* Lowers cholesterol in the body

* Lower blood pressure in the body

* Quickens reaction time to doing things

* Calms emotional stress

* Makes the mind work more efficiently by sending off neurotransmitters from the brain faster

* Helps one concentrate better in all areas of his or her life

* Improves the brain wave and blood flow

* Gives you a sense of contentment with your life

* Gives one the bigger picture of their life and what direction their life is heading in

* Helps the body heal by dropping the brain down into the Alpha brain wave state

* Unblocks the energy centers in one's body.

This energy in the body is called Prana, C'hi, Chi (chee) and Ki

* Helps heal the body through unblocking the Chakras which are the 7 energy centers of the body

The 7 Chakras or energy centers of the body are:

The Root Chakra

The Naval Chakra

The Solar Plexus Chakra

The Heart Chakra

The Throat Chakra

The Third Eye Chakra

The Crown Chakra

* Can bring spirituality or insight and information from The Universe to one's life and give one answers to all of his/her questions concerning health, money, relationships and spiritual knowledge.

V. How to do Meditation

What to Wear

Simply wear clothes that you feel comfortable in. If you can wear the same outfit every time this is even better as every thing you do in a ritual helps your brain remember that you are ready to do that meditation and puts your mind and body into the perfect alpha state for the meditation. Breathing is the most important part of meditation as it oxygenates your entire body and brings oxygen to many places that usually don't get much with your regular shallow breathing you do during most of your day.

How long to Meditate

Do meditation for 20 minutes for each session daily or 30 minutes for each session if you decide to do meditation a few times a week. The important thing is to meditate over the time. If you have no time to meditate due to your busy schedule then doing a 10 minute meditation would be better then not doing it at all. Ideally though 20 minutes is the best to fully experience the most benefits from meditation.

How to Breathe

Prana is an energy that emits from all physical matter and also from the human body. This energy is taken into the body from the human breath.

On a count of four seconds(1-2-3-4) inhale deeply from your root chakra (sex organ area) all the way up to your head (crown chakra) then hold for another count of 4 seconds then release slowly with a count of 4 seconds the air from your crown chakra to your root chakra. Keep repeating this again over and over. After a while you will be able to do this without having to move your diaphragm so much.

How to do Meditation

Sit upright on the floor with your back straight to allow the best energy flow through your body. Touch your 1st finger with your thumb finger on each hand. The key with everything in meditation is to keep it simple so you can use your intention to focus on what information you are getting from Source about ways to improve your life. Simply follow the ritual in the back of this book step by step and you will be able to easily do the meditation. There is an opening prayer at the start of the meditation which allows you to feel better as it calls in powerful Angels and beneficial spirit energies to raise your vibration to a higher vibrational state so you can access this all knowing Source energy better for the best insight possible into your life. There is a chakra meditation that is part of the meditation as well as this will open up your chakras which are your energy centers so you can have your energy flowing easily throughout your body which has many amazing health benefits in itself. There is also a visual meditation to help you connect to your spirit guides and get direct answers to your questions concerning your life. There are also many other meditations in this book to do as well and just do the ones you feel drawn to do.

VI. Types of Meditation

Summary of Types of Meditation

Meditation on the Eastern Tattvas

Meditation on Colors

Meditation on Mantras

Meditation on Mandalas

Meditation on the Elements

Meditation on the Eastern Tattvas

Dharana is the Sanskrit word for the technique of focusing on a single object or point of concentration. These elemental symbols are great symbols to easily keep your focus on for a meditation. The symbols are the shapes of a ***square, a triangle, a circle, a half moon*** and ***an egg shape***. Simply focus on one of these symbols in your mind and keep the symbol in focus for as long as you can. If your mind wanders then just bring it back to that shape again and again until your massage time is finished.

Sit in an upright position so your back is straight and touch your 1st finger with your thumb finger on each hand. Light a candle(s) and sandalwood incense. Set the time for 20 minutes and focus all of your senses and attention on the Tattva you decide to work with.

Meditation on Colors

Sit in an upright position so your back is straight and touch your 1st finger with your thumb finger on each hand. Light a candle(s) and sandalwood incense. Set the time for 20 minutes and focus all of your senses and attention on the Color you decide to work with.

The Colors and their Meanings

Red = Strength and Power

Orange = Vitality and Energy

Yellow = Awareness and Clarity

Green = Growth

Blue = Calmness of Emotions

Purple = Spiritual Insight and Psychic Abilities

White = Enlightenment and Positive Energy

Meditation on Mantras

Sit in an upright position so your back is straight and touch your 1st finger with your thumb finger on each hand. Light a candle(s) and sandalwood incense. Set the time for 20 minutes and focus all of your senses and attention on the Mantra you decide to work with. You can find many books that have many different Mantras in them. A Mantra is a spiritual syllable from the Sanskrit language. They send out physical vibrations which help focus the person into the meditative state.

Mantras and their Meanings

Aum Namah Shivaya (Aum and salutations to Lord Shiva)

Aum Namo Narayanaya (Aum and salutations to the Universal God Vishnu)

Aum Shri Ganeshaya Namah (Aum and salutations to Shri Ganesha)

Meditation on Mandalas

Sit in an upright position so your back is straight and touch your 1st finger with your thumb finger on each hand. Light a candle(s) and sandalwood incense. Set the time for 20 minutes and focus all of your senses and attention on the Mandala you decide to work with. You can find many books that have many different kinds of Mandalas. Here is one for you to try out.

The Peace Mandala (on the next page)

Meditation on the Elements

Sit in an upright position so your back is straight and touch your 1st finger with your thumb finger on each hand. Light a candle(s) and sandalwood incense. Set the time for 20 minutes and focus all of your senses and attention on the Element you decide to work with.

The Elements and their Meanings

Air = Face East direction and meaning information and knowledge

Water = Face West direction and meaning emotions and love

Earth = Face North direction and meaning money and business

Fire = Face South direction and meaning passion and energy

VII. The Zen Buddhist Meditaton Ritual

The Zen Buddhist Meditation

2,500 years ago a man named Siddhartha Gautama (Buddha) practiced meditation over and over and eventually attained Enlightenment. He developed a system to where others could do the same as he did. The Buddha taught moderation and 8 steps to Enlightenment. Zen is the Japanese form of Buddhism that has been adapted by the Western world for Enlightenment.

The 8 Steps to Enlightenment

Right Understanding

Right Thought

Right Speech

Right Action

Right Livelihood

Right Effort

Right Mindfulness

Right Connection

Temple Set up

Set up your altar with your cloth on it and light the candle(s) and sandalwood incense on it as well

Wear lose ritual clothes so you feel comfortable

Record the visual meditation into your digital recorder

Turn off all electronic devices that will distract you

Go to a room that has no noises or distractions

Sit in an upright position so your back is perfectly straight as this allows for the energy to flow through your Chakras and body much better

Set the timer for 20 minutes for your daily meditation session

Touch your 1st finger with your thumb finger on each hand.

There is a Chakra meditation to do first to open up your energy centers or Chakras before you do the meditation.

There is also a visual meditation to do after that which is powerful as it keeps the conscious chatter mind busy and allows you to easily access the subconscious mind for that all knowing Source information

Don't worry about trying to relax before the meditation as by the time you go through this ritual you will be relaxed as it is designed to put the mind into the Alpha state brain wave activity just by going through all the steps.

Don't be discouraged if you can't stay focused during the meditation as practice will make perfect for you and in time this will be very easy for you to do.

Keep a pad and pen near you to write down ideas and insights that come to you after the meditation is done as well as to follow the exercises requested to do in the visual meditation.

Opening Rituals

Ring Bell-*"this temple is now open"*

Take 3 deep breaths and hold for 3 seconds and release

Trance (count down 1 to 30)

Opening Prayer:
*"I am a completion and piece of the puzzle connected to Source.
I feel the flow of energy running through me all the time from Source energy and allow it to flow freely to give me thoughts and ideas, feelings and emotions, sounds and songs, and dreams and visions to improve my life.
I tune in to Source every day to bless me with this flow of love and information.
I let go and follow the guidance I get from Source throughout my days and life.
I have understanding of what others are going through and smile at them when I see them and show compassion and love towards them.
I feel abundance in every part of my life as I continue to trust and follow the daily guidance I get from Source.
I have courage to do the things that I want to do in my life as Source gives me this inner strength.
I feel love towards others and attract it back into every part of my life.
I know that we are all nothing but pure photons or energy and so this allows me to create my reality the way*

that I have always dreamed about.

I am a part of the greater total that is part of Source.

I feel silence and peace echo thorough out every cell in my body and radiate it thorough out the heavens.

I see the innocence and beauty in nature and all around me and mirror that feeling inside of myself.

I keep my life simple so I can experience every great thing that comes along my path.

I understand that we all sense life through our five senses and create a map of our reality and that my map is different from everyone else's map of reality so I allow others to have their morality and ethics just as I have mine.

I comprise only one grain of sand along the vast seashores of the world and feel connected to the Source in this way.

I always trust Source to lead me down each path that is best for me and my life.

I always feel Source is around even when I am alone.

I am aware of subtle energies around me and can easily sense them with my psychic sense of knowing, feeling, hearing and seeing.

I feel guidance in my life from Source and can always call upon Source for any help I need at any time by just closing my eyes and asking my question and then listening for the answer.

I am on an exciting path of adventure as I trust Source in every area of my life.

I feel peace with everyone and everything around me as I have Source in my life to rely upon.

I let Source control my life as Source always has the best path for me take at any point in my life.

I see my life flowering and blossoming as I receive gifts of abundance from Source.

I am wise and knowledgeable as I get all my insight from Source.

I am ok with being in the no-thingness or the void as this gives me quiet time in my life before my next adventure.

I see many possibilities all around me and listen to Source to guide me for the best choice to take.

I celebrate my life and happiness that I have found in each part of my life.

I always participate in life with other people as this makes my life and their life smoother.

I feel harmony in my world and it feels good.

I see success in every part of my life and it makes me happy.

I am grateful of my past as it has made me who I am today.

I am traveling through life and spreading love and light as I am guided by Source.

I am friendly to all that come through my path and if I don't like their energy then I let them pass by and send love and light their way.

Source is everything and everywhere and is nothing but pure white light.

I am always patient with people just as Source is always patient with me.
I am experiencing life to the fullest as Source guides me.
I enjoy my life moment to moment and experience its beauty.
I like being playful at times.
I am integrating into everything around me.
I feel healed from Source and heal others with my thoughts and feelings.
I enjoy sharing with others just as Source keeps sharing with me.
I am a wise master teacher and a wise master student as well.
I feel the intensity of life and enjoy it.
I am receptive to information that comes through me from life and Source.
I am a co-creator with the great Universe out there.
I feel creativity in every part of my life and let it flow through me.
I welcome change in all parts of my life as I know Source just keeps bringing me better and better things.
I am constantly allowing my mind to expand to higher vibrations that are coming through my body.
Source is the creator of us all.
I hear my inner voice and always follow it as it leads me to greater and greater things.
I am aware and conscious of Source energy all around me and inside of me as it enlightens me.

I call upon the energies of the great avatars. Source, Jesus Christ, Buddha, Krishna, Rama, Osiris, Quan Yin, Hermes Trismegist, Zoroaster, Moses, Muhammad, Orpheus, Lao-Tzu, Confucius, Helena Roerich, Helena Blavatsky, Baha' Ullah, Tsongkhapa, Shankara, Mahavira, Manjushri and Guru Nanak. I call upon the great Gods of ancient Greece, Rome, Celtic, Nordic, Egyptian and Babylonian civilizations. I call upon the Archangels Raphael, Gabriel, Michael and Auriel. I call upon Metatron and Sandalphon. I call upon the YHVH (yode-hey-vavh-hey). I call upon all the Saints. I call upon the great Galactic beings out in the Universe, the Sun, the Moon, the Star, the Planets, Mother Earth and the entire Solar System who support me and my efforts and to raise all of life to light and love and fill all of our hearts with compassion and love. I call upon my I AM presence to bring my offerings of light and love to create clarity, divine direction and love manifestation in all that I do.
I AM that I AM.

Opening the Chakras Meditation

Sit in an upright position so your back is straight. Focus on the Chakra area and touch your 1st finger with your thumb finger and vibrate this Sanskrit word to open up the chakra. Also visualize the color in a ball moving in a clockwise direction in that chakra area. Do this for each Chakra listed in the order below. Do this for a minute or so for each Chakra until you can feel or see this energy clearly.

Root Chakra: (where your sex organs are at)
Color: Red
Sanskrit word: LAM

Naval Chakra: (between your sex organ and belly button)
Color: Orange
Sanskrit word: VAM

Solar Plexus Chakra: (where your stomach is)
Color: Yellow
Sanskrit word: RAM

Heart Chakra: (where your heart is)
Color: Green
Sanskrit word: YAM

Throat Chakra: (where your throat is)
Color: Blue
Sanskrit word: HAM

Third Eye Chakra: (where your forehead is)
Color: Purple
Sanskrit word: OM

Crown Chakra: (the top of your head)
Color: White
Sanskrit word: OM

Visual Meditation

Write down any questions that you have about your life in areas of money, health, relationships and spirituality that you want answers to. The more specific the questions you ask the more specific the answers will be so be very specific with your questions!

Sit in an upright position and keep your notepad and pen near you and be ready to write when you are finished with this meditation.

(Record this portion into a recorder one time to use over and over again)

Visualize yourself walking down a smooth path and as you are walking you come up to a castle door that is a very tall medieval door. The door has a 5 pointed star on it with the point pointing up to the sky. You instantly get the thought that this is a pentagram and the pentagram symbol pointing up means that Spirit is above us and is a good thing. And the other points represent water, air, fire and earth or the four elements. This pentagram is used for protection and will protect you as you are inside your sanctuary. Only good spirits can enter this sanctuary with this large pentagram pointing upwards on the door. This door is a secret door that only you have access to. There are no walls around this door as this is a spiritual opening to the spirit world and your sanctuary where

you will feel safe and happy. You reach into your pocket and take out a large and beautiful golden key that lights up as you unlock the door. The door immediately unlocks and you open the handle and push open the door open. You see the most beautiful meadow you have ever seen in your life and can not wait to enter your sanctuary! You close the door and start walking on the path which has some soft freshly cut grass on it. You can smell the fresh scent of the grass as you walk on it. You feel relaxed and safe here as this is your sanctuary and nobody else has access to this hidden sanctuary of yours. Every time you go to your sanctuary will feel all your stress leave your mind and body. You also will feel very happy and all your troubles will instantly disappear. This sanctuary will make you feel very safe and protected and allows you to feel free to open up your heart and mind as there are only safe beneficial spirits here that can help and protect you. It is a warm summer day and the sun is bright and you can feel the sun's warm glow upon your skin. You see a very tall tree ahead in the distance and you decide to walk towards the tree as you almost can hear it calling to you to come closer to it. This is the only tree in your sanctuary and it's the tallest tree you have ever seen in your life! It seems as if this tree reaches so far into the sky that it touches the heavens. You are very excited about walking to this tree to experience its energy. As you get closer to the tree you hear the sounds of birds chirping in the sky and it's as if they are singing a song as they fly. The birds are the most beautiful multi-colored birds you have ever seen in your life and you enjoy watching them. You feel warm and comfortable and all of your body feels so relaxed and good as you continue to get closer to the tree. As you get closer to the tree you notice a small alter on the right side of the path. On the altar is a small yellow corn basket with 2 pieces of fruit on it and a little sign that has your name on it as if to tell you that this fruit is for you! You take the fresh strawberry and put it into your mouth. This is the sweetest and best strawberry you have ever tasted in your life and you savor every bite from it. You now take the piece of green apple out of the basket and put this into your mouth and really enjoy the tanginess of this in your mouth. You close your eyes for a minute and enjoy chewing on this apple savoring every bite. You now feel nourished and happy and continue to walk to the tree which is only a few steps away now. You take a few more steps and are now at the tree and feeling calm, happy and satisfied. You instantly feel that there is someone behind the tree that wants to talk to you and are excited about what they have to tell you. You sense that it is a good spirit that wants to give you information about your life. The spirit walks out from behind the tree to greet you. You listen to the spirit talk for a while and then ask questions. Now open your eyes and take your pen and paper out and write about what you saw, felt, heard or just knew about the spirit that talked to you. Then start writing what comes into your mind-don't think! Just keep writing! No punctuation or complete thought is necessary-just keep the pen writing on anything that comes to your mind and you will get insight from Source on your life. (Turn off the recorder now)

The Zen Buddhist Meditation

Sitting in an upright position with your back and spine straight and eyes closed and touch your 1st finger with your thumb finger and think about these logic puzzles to get your mind in the flow of this Zen Buddhist Meditation. Also feel free to ask any questions about your life in areas of money, health, relationships and spirituality that you want answers to. Ask these questions in your mind or out loud before you start the logic puzzles. Keep a pad and pencil nearby so after this meditation you can write down any answers you get. The answers also may come in the next few hours or days so pay attention to thoughts etc. that pop into your head without having to logically think about them. And always follow these thoughts etc. as these will improve your life!

Zen Buddhist Logic Puzzles:

* What is the sound of both hands clapping?

* Where do you go from the top of a tree?

* How does a big bird escape from a long-necked bottle?

* Can and animal attain enlightenment?

* If you are hanging by your teeth to a branch over a waterfall and someone comes along and asks you a question, do you answer them?

* What is the meaning of life?

* Visualize how far Source energy reaching throughout the Universe

* Feel how much love would be in the world if everyone was happy

* Listen to all the birds flying by in your imaginary world

* What does I AM that I AM mean to you?

* What would it feel like throughout your day if you felt nothing but positive thoughts, positive conversations and emails?

Closing Rituals

In the next day or two you will get *thoughts and ideas, feelings and emotions, sounds and songs, dreams and visions* about your life and ways to improve it so **follow all of these thoughts etc. as these are your answers from the spiritual world!**

Remember just like anything in life *Practice Makes Perfect!* If you want to be great at these meditations and feel the energy while you are doing the meditations as well as to get answers to your questions from the meditation then do this meditation often! Doing this meditation every day or a few times a week will bring peace and calmness into your life, increase your energy and focus for your daily busy life and bring better health, success and happiness to your life in every possible way!

Moving Towards Enlightenment

Meditation can create a breakthrough in your life to where you can sense the world around you better, get insight from The Universe or Source as to how to live your life better, feel like your energy is flowing better and make you feel happier and invigorated in every part of your life. All your energy towards spirituality (not religion) and positive energy eventually leads to becoming Enlightened. You will know when you become Enlightened because you will feel at one with The Universe.
Blessings to you,
Kuriakos

Check out more of the Author's book at www.Kuriakos.biz

The Zen Buddhist Meditation Journal

The Zen Buddhist Meditation Journal

The Zen Buddhist Meditation Journal

868994

Printed in Great Britain by
Amazon.co.uk, Ltd.,
Marston Gate.